Sickness
Poetry by Jessica Burby

by

Jessica Burby

DORRANCE
PUBLISHING CO
EST. 1920
PITTSBURGH, PENNSYLVANIA 15235

Dorrance Publishing Co
585 Alpha Drive
Pittsburgh, PA 15238
Visit our website at www.dorrancebookstore.com

ISBN: 979-8-8860-4250-4
eISBN: 979-8-8860-4521-5

Introduction

This collection of poems I wrote is very personal. They express my deepest fears, cares, regrets, and torment I have gone through in my life so far. These poems help me release all this turmoil I go through. You could think of my writing as an equivalent to journaling, or whatever a person would use to vent emotion. These poems may seem "negative," but they are actually a very positive healthy thing for dealing with depression or any ailment.

A House on A Hill 1.11.2009

There is a house that sits on a hill
It sits there quiet and still
But inside this house
Lives a pain
That swirls around everyone's brain
Trying to drive them insane
It's a never-ending game
And everyone is to blame

This dark curse
Completes every mistake
We are bound to make
Which makes us all horribly fake
And that
Is something I can't take.

<u>Living Broken Bone</u> 3.23.2010

I'm torn
I'm scorned
I'm a living broken bone
I thought I was breaking a mold
But now
Why should I go on?
I'm living, but not alive
I need to break my disguise

Fear is swallowing every element of me
And taking my right to breathe
It feels like torture
An overwhelming pressure
It lives inside
In your subconscious mind
Did I survive?

Miserable Earth 4.1.2010

Will I always be forced
To walk upon this miserable earth
Alone and afraid
Just praying to be saved
Barely getting through every day
Picking apart my tortured brain
Until there's nothing left to explain.

I Need 4.2.2010

I need help
I need to flee
Oh God, this feels like insanity
It seems they're trying to break me
But that's all I've ever seen
I can't let this bother me
It pulls me down like gravity

There is no choice
I don't have a voice
Everything is noise

These frantic words
Kill me to the core
It's always either; or
This is very hard to ignore

To Be Free

The only way
For me
To be
Free
Is separating from
What is mentally hindering me

I can't define the delusion
Or
Confusion
I'm lost
It makes me soft
And I forget what's best
This is so much stress
It feels like a test

But
It's a delusion
So why the confusion?
See,
It's absolution
Taken from inside me
Thrown all around me
What can this be?
I need to be free

To Create a Monster

My Blood:
It pours
Screaming:
No More
What have you got in store?

This is all I'm against
Who wouldn't take offense?
I will taste my blood
I will do this in love
I will show what's true
I will show you what you really knew

To Hell with your test
I will always be blessed

There is NO giving in
That's not where I end or begin
Why would you want this?
Walking on earth
Why would you create
Something that ruins fate
Something so morbid
Now, the day I dread
I want darkness instead.

What I Am

What I truly believe
Is not
What you've seen

Violence, screaming
None is needed
By fighting against
I became bent

I lost my soul
I lost control
I'm truly tame
I'm partially to blame

I could've been smarter
I could've realized
I'm a monster
Lost as a Martyr
Thinking it didn't matter

I was right
But I made it wrong
I took away where I belong
Now,
I'm no longer strong

Waging War

I'm waging war upon myself
And the daily struggle of this hell
It's monotonous
I can tell
Yet,
Different
To say the least
Not normal
Not me

When will this end?
I can no longer pretend
It hurts
This is getting worse
It's not normally how I'm living
These symptoms I can't take
These symptoms I need to break

The Fire

The fire illuminates
It gives and it takes
The fire burns
It's screaming:
LEARN!

The fire surrounds you
Enticing you
Beating you
Meeting you
Turning you
Keeping you cool
Always knowing your next move
How can this be understood?
I was never meant to belong
The slicing stars
Are leaving shards of my life
Broken
Under the knives
And each knife has a name
Would it be right to blame?

A Mental Struggle

Get out, Get out, Get out
I think
I'm about to choke
You're not the one I pick
You're as dirty as a snake

This obsession is taxing
You're not a blessing
You're not what I'm requesting
I'm running so far
You will never be a scar
I'm cold and hard
Praying to be justified
With all these lies
You should know by now
I can't be held down

The Illness 3.3.2017

The illness entices me
Screaming, come along please
The illness breaks me
Leaves me empty
Scares me in and out of reality

I guess it doesn't matter
My brain is scattered
It won't focus
I'm losing touch
What have I done?

<u>The Veil</u> 4.1.2017

The veil falls
I go in and out
The reality
I thought
Just twinkles and sparks

I sob
Feeling robbed

Uncontrollable tears
Help me feel
The years
All piled into one
Crushing everything I once was.

<u>Funny Story</u> 4.3.2017

Their blinded minds
And cursing lies
Trap me with what feels like vines
Wrapping around from all sides
Stealing away my conscious mind

Twisting it and turning it
Until I'm rendered blind

Then
As I fell
They decided it was just a funny story to tell

No
Caring or compassion
Just absurd laughing

Their torturing, distorted faces
Bring me to unknown places
Obscure delusions
With unknown conclusions
Just bring torture and hate
Like it's bringing me to fate.

People Break 4.15.2017

Sometimes people break
But it's alright
Because,
This snake
Can't help but take
Everything from me
There's no way for anyone to see
How could anyone believe
This is my PTSD
Something you can't see
It's torturing me

I look insane
But he's to blame
It's always about looks
Not what he took
Not reality
Will anyone ever believe?

<u>Beautiful Delusions</u> 1.14.2018

It's a wonderland
A masterful plan

Beauty with every song
Lifting my mind
Ending my time
Exposing my lies
Or
Their lies

Which is it?
I'm confused
So consumed
I don't know what to do
How will I get through?
What am I supposed to do?

<u>Excitement Control</u> 1.28.2018

My brain is losing control
Why can't it just be good?

Is it too much stimulation?
And my brain can't take it?

The excitement felt so good
I didn't know I'd lose my brain's control
But now I'm delusional
It seems like a mistake
To light up that part of my brain
I thought it to be an outlet
To get out my excitement
However,
I ruined it.

A Wolf in Disguise 1.29.2018

A wolf in sheep's clothing
And you act chosen
I'm shocked with disbelief
Stricken with grief
At your cruelty

Why do the good
Not do as they should
And only be cruel
To those who needs the fuel

Fuel for their lives
For their hearts to thrive
And continue to survive

The people set apart
Are not always
What I thought
I'll proceed with caution
So, I don't go to the grave
As a lost one.

Naïve Eve 1.29.2018

Women may be naïve
Just like Eve
But our hearts and minds will bleed
When the effects of our mistakes are seen
Our hearts are big
And we grieve
All you consider to be caused by Eve

Evil,
When we commit
We will feel and usually admit

Our hearts and souls
Have bled too long
With all the punishment
For men,
It belongs

They're mean
They're cruel
They've never understood
They don't pay for their mistakes
They've made
So, women will suffer
No matter what is done or uttered

I Won't Turn Away 1.29.2018

This is how you turn people from Christianity
By being cruel and mistaken
By acting like things are only as your thinking
But I won't turn away
No matter who you blame
You are not God
You have not seen all

Your opinion on my life
Is obnoxious
Complete nonsense
You've been around me a short time
You do not know my life
And to the person that started this mess
Of a thought process
Thank you,
It's for my very best.

<u>Fear Won't Leave</u> 1.29.2018

I'm completely scared
Feeling nothing but terror
If it was real
I know they'd kill

My laughter is good while it lasts
Since depression fills my past
But my looming dark fears come back
That this could be reality's attack

I'm glad it's not real
It's too frightening to feel
So many dangerous options
On how they'd get back at my opinions
It torments me so extremely
It can't be real
But I'm still overwhelmed with fear

A Fantasy 1.29.2018

It should've stayed a fantasy
But then came insanity
It weakened me
Made me do things
I truly find wrong
It's not what I want

Now there's nothing but disgust
Between us
No more lust
Just things to forget
In order to not regret

I set out with a purpose
But it all became confusion
It was due to underlying emotions

I didn't really know how I felt
Until I messed it up
It's too late now
At least he didn't really get my heart
I know
I stopped that part.

Shine on my Face 2.1.2018

The sun shines on my face
I never want to leave this place
It's a beautiful escape
Bringing a wondrous mind state

The warmth I feel
Has got to heal
All this pain
This never-ending rain
That's meant to drive me insane
With the devil's weaselly ways
And now I have traded my days
Of warming sun
That would've brought love

Beautiful Water 2.3.2018

The beautiful water rolls in
And I feel free from my pain
I just focus in
And peace begins
A beautiful emptiness
Fills my stage
And all I view are never-ending waves
It captures my brain
Finally,
In a positive way
This brings warmth to my face
And I feel unconditionally saved.

A Plague 2.12.2018

I pay for my happiness
Not ever,
A full day can I miss
Without anger or tears
He sends everyone into fear

He's a hypocrite
Telling lies
Manipulating my why's
He's a plague, like flies

In appearance, he's a lie
He has a master disguise
It sends me into a spiral
He's conniving and evil
It's frightening
Who could love him?
I don't understand.

Daybreak 2.13.2018

Daybreak comes
And the sting has just begun

The blinding sun
Has a light
That brings an odd fright
Most people enjoy the day
But that's when I feel most insane

The peace of the night
Keeps me calm and mentally light

The day breaks
With torturous pain
Oh, another day
Will I be the same?
Or even okay?

I can only pray
And try not to be the same
Just as all the other days.

Past Attack 2.15.2018

The past attacks
How do I fight back?
All I know
Is to react
I can't, I can't
I'm losing control
I need something good to grab hold
The sting of the cold
Throws my soul
Into a never-ending hold

A Fight.
Evil or light?
Please Lord,
Help me win
Please Lord,
Help this end!

A Time of Doubt 2.19.2018

God is a fraud
He does not make you strong
He puts you on your knees
And you will always bleed

The blood will pour out of you
Never ceasing to kill you
Never will you feel renewed

Life is so much clearer
Without the spiritual
Not as much fear
Bringing me to tears

I've wasted so many years
With a false hope
Destroying my life and future
Taking sanity out of the picture
Not everything is better
But the spiritual delusions can no longer
Torture.

<u>Bloody Words</u> 3.17.18

Blood is pouring
My words are flowing
All I see are crimson drops
As out of my mind floods the thoughts
Streaming around the page
The blood-filled words
Calm the rage
These words bring peaceful rest to life
But let the pain flow
To end it right
To end my fight
The conclusion to this demented night.

Take a Stay 5.8.2018

Come take a stay in my mind
You won't believe what you find
The torture and the pain
Mixed with shame
It never ends
Is it all pretend?

It won't even take a break
It consumes
Makes me a fuse
Waiting to blow
Falling into the unknown

It's like a show
With unknown intentions
A mystery
That makes me question my sanity
Along with my vanity

My life is in ruins
I can no longer pursue it
My life, my dreams
All of it's lost to me
Where lies my futures key
Where's that breakthrough
Can I ever push through?

<u>The Truth</u> 5.20.2018

Denying the truth in me
Got me to where you see
This pathetic existence
Barely realizing
This is an obsession
That was always unhealthy
No wonder, it brought insanity
If you can admit it
You can fix it
If you deny there's something
Wrong in you
It'll still find a way through
Through, the disguise
And you'll continue to lie

And it's only to yourself
So, how can you be helped?
Learn to admit to yourself.

Tortured Road 5.20.2018

I've been traveling on my tortured road
Scared of everything I've come to know
Let alone
Everything I don't
The scars are tearing apart,
My will to love anyone
It doesn't matter
Who you are
There will always be distance
Whether you're aware or not
Sometimes I won't be caught
The illusion will be strong
They won't know
They don't know
So,
The real me can lay dormant
While I fool you into believing
What I'm not.

Deep Seeded Cold 5.20.2018

I now realize
I want that unconditional love
That comes from that truly special one
Yet,
Am I capable of changing from
What I was?

This mindset
Of independence and bitterness
Is all I know
Will I always be this cold?
Will I ever open my heart?
Will I ever change my part?
Is it worth it?
Will it only ruin me?

Well,
I probably won't break through
So,
To love me would be a waste for you
I can't be true
To a heart so bruised

My heart broke years ago
I can't let it go
There is no way back from this
Deep seeded cold
So,
I will stay alone.

A Musical Battle Ground 5.22.2018

A passion concealed
Throughout the years
Can engulf you in fear
And breaking through
Can seem the hardest thing to do

It brought me insanity
Because it opened me
And I began to believe
It's okay to feel

But it was too much
Because it was suppressed
It brought thoughts
That should've been stopped
Now, it's too late
And the enemy took its place.

Where I Land 5.22.2018

I'm not just looking for fun
But I don't know about love
It exists for some
But, will I ever meet
The right one
Has my life just begun?

This new way of thinking
Has me wondering
Will it happen for me?
Does God think it's what I need?
Ultimately,
His plan
Is where I want to land.

Overcome with Fear 5.27.2018

I was overcome with fear
So, I made a mistake
That was detrimental
My faith was not found
In that moment of decision
I lost my life's vision

Being scared of things getting worse
Caused my soul to feel cursed
Before and afterwards
I felt disturbed
It was not true to your word.
Or my soul
I long for what's pure
Not the darkness I gave control.

Meant More Than You Knew 5.27.2018

That semester with all of you
Meant more than you knew
I was so broken and bruised
I found something true
Even though I was lost and confused

You showed me I mattered
You showed me there was still good
You brightened my life
Even just for a time
Thank you,
For being kind
Even though things are now
Different
I will never forget.

<u>Why?</u> 5.27.2018

My blood,
It Pours
Screaming:
NO MORE!

Are you scared?
Are you dared?
Do you believe?
What I see?

What are you doing?
Do you think it's funny?
Taking all from me?

Twisting who I am
Into black sand
While I just wait to wash away
Inevitably the tide will come
And there is no more sun

I'll always be trapped in the dark
How do I even start?
To mend these wounds
These unnatural scars
That you've put in my heart
I can't even pretend

My brain is twisting and turning
Even yearning
To turn reality to confusion
Now,
I'm lost in poison.
Now,
My life's been dismissed.

Luckily 5.27.2018

Luckily, it didn't go far
Luckily, I know who you are
Luckily, your ignorance took hold
And no one took me in from the cold

That is not what I needed
I need to be self-sufficient
No man, needs to love me
At least romantically
You will see,
Eventually
My words were true
But not by what you knew.
You'd never understand
You don't dig deep in the sand
You just stand above
Have you ever been selfless
Enough to love?
I knew you wouldn't accept me
Even if, I made you believe a lie about me
So, it is what you believe
And I am free.

Intertwined 5.27.2018

The devil is
Intertwined
In my mind
Stealing focus
It's hocus pocus
Just ridiculous

The evil is there
I'm completely scared
It's consuming, torturing
Never-ending
It's terrifying
So, what's keeping me from crying
At least more than I do?
This is far from understood
I wish I could
He just pounds on my brain
Taking my weakness
And driving me insane
With my longing to love
That won't change
But, never again
Will I get that desperate
It changed my fate
Now, what awaits?

Their Torture 6.2.2018

There's only so much I can take
Waiting for fate
The twinkling stars
Fall from afar

Falling from my head
Anticipating my death
The unknown scream
Can't hardly be
When, their torture exists
It's hard to resist
But can't be missed

It seems so real
Will I heal?

How can I know reality?
When my mind is spinning
My mind is lost and has little control
It's an empty black hole
Or so I'm told
While waiting for more
I'm told,
I'm always on the defense
Just waiting for the Lord's presence
To free me completely
From this torturous symphony.

The Warmth of the Ocean 7.10.2018

The warmth shines down on me
The roar of the ocean calms me
It brings beautiful understanding
Of the joys of living

The sun sparkling on the water
Reminds me of grace
When I falter
It's a never-ending glow
Helps me feel at home

The feeling in my mind
Takes away my strife
For a moment I'm in bliss
And in moments like this
I understand I want to live.

Heart Filled Writing 8.3.2018

These poems I wrote
Are more than works of art
They come straight from my tortured heart
The hole inside tears me apart
The hidden love
Is more than they know
I care more than I'm able to show
People have taken advantage
Of what they know
What would they do then?
With what I won't show
This vulnerability,
You will only see
In my writing

You cannot break me
This concrete wall
Can never fall
I can't be free
Because others will use me.

Illusions of Ghosts 8.3.2018

Illusions in my mind
Turn into ghosts from my past
That are laughing through the dance
The dance in my mind
Is a strategic lie
A self-sabotaging game
Making me lose my way
Making it a struggle to be sane.

<u>So Sad</u> 8.9.2018

Why do I long for something I never had?
It's so sad
Not,
Because I never had it
But,
Because I want it

How can this be?
I just want to be free
This emptiness is too much
I shouldn't need to be loved
At least romantically
I don't want this
It's not bliss
It shouldn't be worth it to me
This I know
So, I bleed
Metaphorically
And I hate this change in me.

Struggling 8.27.2018

I'm struggling to know my worth
In a life that seriously hurts
Everything is heartbreaking
Knocking the wind out of me
My vision is darkness
I can't seem to break through this
To find what's good
It won't be understood

I feel like nothing
It won't stop thundering
It's extremely startling
Unearthing martyrdom
That should not have been sung
This state of mind I've been in
Always makes me a victim

But, is it truth?
No,
I misunderstood
Why does the darkness continue through?
Why can't I change this mood?
Where's my conscious effort?
That will make life worth it?

Lack of Love 8.31.2018

A lack of love
Caused me to scream
To whatever lives above
The pain within
Caused my brain to spin

And no one ever showed up
To help me mend this insane
Crutch

All I needed...
But,
I'm still bleeding

I'm only human
And I do have feelings
Although I hide it
And try not to be consumed
By it
Love is terrifying
Anyone could do anything
It would hurt too much
My heart,
It can't touch.

Grounding Control 9.11.2018

He surrounds my mind
But disappears
With just a flick of hand
Literally just a movement
Takes you out of a delusion
Brings you back to what you're pursuing

This technique
Has always been helpful to me
But,
Back to the symptom

This feels like a battle ground
Like he's trying to bring me down
Pulling me down to the ground
If it's real
He's a coward
Now, I'm not grounded
I need to find what's real again
I go in and out of thoughts
And I fear they're all bought
Oh, Lord
Here I go
And I fear there's no control.

Stealing My Time 9.11.2018

Insecurities could ruin me
I can never seem to break free
They're constantly stealing my time
While I become paralyzed
And scared of life

It's kind of calming
It's a feeling
While twisting and diluting
My mind
It steals my time

It's a scary dream
And I can't scream
Why do you want to torture me?
Why would I believe?
I can't conceive
Why you'd ruin me.

Numbing Memories 9.16.2018

It doesn't seem real to me
The mistakes I've seen
I'm numb
Yet, bleeding
My mind is exploding
The embarrassment I can't see
The feeling is blocked for me
It's for the best though
Because numbness leaves me still whole
I have to be in control
I slipped up too much
I wasn't conscious
　　　of what would be torturous
A disturbance in me took hold
I was out of control
But I'm working through that horrific mold.

<u>A Lack</u> 9.18.2018

The beauty of the insane
Came from a lack in my brain
Or maybe
From my heart
But, isn't the brain where it starts?

The technical reality
Of what I've been missing
Makes me wonder
Is this why I'm going under?

My brain is to blame
My heart took the pain
Shattered me all the way
Changing my not fully formed brain
Into something
It should've never became.

Music 9.21.2018

A weight lifts
At a certain sound
It's a precious gift
It's light and softened
And I feel it.

Hardness Flowing 9.21.2018

A hardness flows through
That issue
I won't get into

It scares me
More than a horror movie
I feel terror at the thought
That someone has stopped

Stopped,
To notice the good unfolding
The mess I'm holding
The strength I'm supporting

I try more than they know
To make my life unfold
It'll take time
To push through this knife
That has stabbed every aspect of my life.

<u>Just Read</u> 10.27.2018

My soul bleeds
Through every page you read
Read this poetry
And you will know me
I go deep
I face it all
No matter how hard

Don't forget my strength
Even through all you take
I will survive my mistakes
And end what's fake

I will find where I should be
With the people that should know me
The ones who understand what I see
And help me become complete.

Dreams of Torment

No one to blame
But my own brain
How long will it attack me?
Will I live like this for eternity?

It never stops tormenting
It's unrelenting

What is reality?
I have no idea of what to believe
It's in my head
Yet, is all I dread
Like, it's real
And will never end
How do I convince myself?
It's only a life I dreamt.

Ink-Stained Getaway 1.18.2019

The ink-stained page
Helps in my getaway
It brings me faith
I have life left to live
It turns severe negative
Into something so positive
The release it gives
Helps me feel fortunate
It reminds me
Life, might not be over for me
That maybe,
I'm good for something.

A Dreams Agony 2.10.2019

I'm agonized
By what's left behind
I want to do it
But,
I know this,
My life could perish.
In a world so morbid
Stealing blissful consciousness
Out of my grasp
Spinning me into an empty abyss
That's hard to miss.

Stuck in the Mundane 2.10.2019

Will I forever be stuck in the mundane?
Just finding ways
To get through the days
While staying completely insane
Contemplating my escape
Tortured by my mistakes

I'm slowly dissolving
Into nothing that's functioning
Clearly drowning

I'm stuck under the dirt
And a shovel hasn't worked
What is typical
Is not what I wished for.

<u>Dreadful Feelings</u> 2.14.2019

Birds fly by my window
And it adds to the paranoia
This dreadful feeling
Is just assuming
A reason more
Then a psychotic process
Stealing my consciousness
And making me delirious
It's gives me a reason for my gun
A very good reason to run.

Strange Feelings 2.14.2019

These feelings are strange
Just completely insane
Why is my brain trying to change?
The way I've felt
Now, the ice is trying to melt

I don't like it
I don't need it
I just need to believe again
That I can function

I don't need a man to heal me
Why am I so crazy?
It's consuming
Making me impulsive
I need to shake this.

Remind Me 2.14.2019

My failures could break me
But Lord,
Help them make me
Lead me, guide me
Gently remind me
There is hope for me

No matter the circumstance
I can find happiness
Fulfill my life
In ways of light

My hope is fading
I can't stand waiting
I don't know how I'll get through
And figure out what to do
Fear has me consumed
How can I break through?
When it feels like I'm just
Entertainment for you.

Hollow Being 3.5.2019

I'm hollow towards human beings
Unless they trigger within
What causes sobbing to begin
This feeling is the truest in me

The sun may shine
But I remain blind
There is no good within
Where is that remarkable feeling?

I live in darkness
Trying to keep myself in tortured bliss
Suffocating my will to live
I need the sun to win.

<u>Angel Faces</u> 3.5.2019

Demons with angel faces
Take your life to dark places
They will turn anything against you
And yet, you're consumed.

Keys 3.5.2019

The keys to my heart
Remain in a note
Tucked away and never shown
People don't know
What drives me and helps
Me grow
It's not time for me to show
Will they ever see?
Well,
It's up to God
Not me.

<u>The Night you Just Smiled</u> 3.5.2019

All you've wanted is to see me cry
That's why you just smiled
I left that night
And could've died
And even then,
You would've smiled

Both of you hurt me
And I don't remember
Why I was crying
But at least she tried
To stop me from risking
My life
An intervention that night
Was influence from the divine
Because even though you stood by
And smiled
Along with me,
God cried.

Why I'm Alive? 3.7.2019

I look to the sky
To see why I'm alive
With all this anguish
You'd think I would end it
At least that's what I see

Will I ever change this song?
The melody of my soul
Is melancholy but bold
Always trying to be sold
Into the abyss of the cold
While I grasp at love
I can't hold.

Writing 3.7.2019

it feels so good to write
it leaves my brain feeling
    light
from all the burdens
I hold onto
it gives me someone to sing
     my song to

it changes what's within me
to a beautiful symphony
of words I believe.

Believe What You Will 3.7.2019

Looks can be deceiving
The lies are receding
Although their cover will last
It's all in the past
So,
Believe what you will
I'll take another pill
Escaping the insanity
Is the only way for me to be free.

<u>Honesty</u> 3.7.2019

Falling
Calling
Screaming for honesty
I'm crawling through life
Just trying to get my head right

I just don't know what to do
With myself
Man,
I'm so unwell
Living out this torturous hell
I'll always need a pill
It's a hard thing to swallow
But reality can never
Come clear
Because some things were real.

<u>Poison</u> 3.10.2019

I can't entertain these feelings
They are like poison
Outrageously ruining
Everything I could be
Everything I will be
This will change me

But the ruin won't last forever
This will not take my treasure
I will get through
What's got me confused
And be made new
Return to myself
And be made well
Escaping this hell

I will stop obsessing
And questioning
And end
The effects
Of this toxin.

Destroying 3.11.2019

All this darkness in my mind
Takes my time
Destroys my passions
Takes reality and twists it
Into unusual abnormalities
That are destroying and disturbing me
They have severe consequences
That render me useless

Losing all I hoped in
Has taken its toll again
I'm always looking within
But still,
I can't begin.

<u>The Game</u> 3.13.2019

I see now
The game was to leave me scarred
The game,
Was to leave me maimed

There's no innocence
Just sly violence
I should've known it

I couldn't see
Every truth in front of me
I fooled myself to believe
You actually cared for me
It was a delusional conspiracy
And I'm left empty.

<u>Quelling Hell</u> 3.27.2019

This has been a nightmare
I'm sick of being scared
I truly hope,
It's not real
Just like I tell myself
To quell this tormenting hell
That leaves me unwell
And changes my judgement
Into foolish impulses
Causing me to act out of
Character
When will the real me return?
All I do is try like hell
Yet,
Nobody can tell.

The Pull of Hell 3.28.2019

It's pulling me in
This twisted hell I live
It's just continuous

My mind is playing with my soul
I'm falling into a torturous show
Covering the chaos
That my brain thinks is a must
Swallowing my life
Sending me into a broken abyss
I was never meant to live.

<u>Curiosity</u> 3.28.2019

I need to hear it
Just to see it
But it's hard to remember
It has nothing to do with me

My brain fools me
Into temporary insanity
Falling into an illusion
That's just confusion

It's like someone's calling me
Trying to help me see
It's a beautiful
Yet,
Torturous reality
Sending shivers to the core of me
It's still hard to believe
It has nothing to do with me.

<u>Mistaken Hatred</u> 3.28.2019

I don't know what's wrong with me
I'm denying reality
Or maybe...
The delusions are taking ahold of me
This curse is swallowing

My mistaken hatred
Towards men I didn't give a chance
As twisted as it is
It's creating an opening
Now I'm longing
To fill a void in me
This hole curses me
Takes my strength
And leaves me pondering

Am I really meant to be lonely?

Black Vines 4.23.2019

Black vines are swirling around my mind
They bring me deep inside
The labyrinth of my mind
I go through corridor after corridor
And find no order
Now,
I'm swirling through my thoughts
Trying to find truthful help
But,
Those blackened vines
Steal what's mine
They send me soaring through
A cold abyss
Never fully knowing what to believe.

Stinging Truth 4.25.2019

It kind of stings
The truth about me
Just lingering
And waiting
For me to bleed

Waiting for the down pour
Of all I try to ignore
The feelings are uncomfortable
But, what am I singing for?
The truth is there
But I can't be fair.

Past Traps 4.25.2019

Focusing on the past
Can lead you into traps
Traps, within your mind
That leave you devastatingly blind
Bits and pieces
Coming like demons
Strangle the truth
Make you confused

Your actions
Won't match what's happening
And truth gets lost
In the emotional crashing.

Beautiful Abyss 5.17.2019

A beautiful abyss
Of pure happiness
Is what I fell into
And I was dazed
But, the ground gave way
And darkness is here to stay
It was just a game
Created by my brain

I would've flown
Into a beautiful unknown
A career,
Would've been there
Now,
All I have is a darkened bliss
That could never reach true love's
Kiss.

<u>I Hate</u> 5.17.2019

I hate what I've done
I hate what I've become
There's nowhere left to run
It's time,
To face the monster,
I've created
With my foolish emotional behavior
I've become
What I fought against
But, it's never what I meant
Things got out of hand
Now once again,
I must rebegin.

<u>Don't Understand</u> 7.17.2019

My brain is intertwined
With truth and lies
 While these fruitful lives
Misunderstand
And remain blind
They can't comprehend
That your mind can bend
Turning you
Into something
You never knew
Just,
Crippling,
Dismantling,
Creating, yet,
Misunderstanding.

<u>Working It Through</u> 9.27.2019

I'm working it through
With every poem you consume
Will this help me get better?
 Or only torment me further?

<u>Trying to Escape</u> 10.9.2019

It's not a physical place
But a torturous state
Is what I'm trying to escape
It's never-ending torture
I'm wondering what I'm living for
But, I don't want to die this time
I want to always try
But, will it end?
Will my soul mend?
These are serious questions
And I don't have the answers
It's a terrifying reality
If there's no escaping
And no real changing
Then I ask again
Why am I living?

Truth of my Soul 1.4.2020

 How does it feel to destroy a life?
Creating a torturous delight
That is meant to kill my light
I spend all my time
Trapped in night
But,
At least no one is there
To be aware
Of the truth my soul needs
To truly believe
Life is worth living.

Losing Control 1/19/2020

Stuck in a fairytale land
I feel I'm losing control to a man
A twisting game in my mind
Making me lose all sense of time

Days blur
My beliefs become obscure
I feel nauseous
Do I need to be cautious?

<u>Divine Design?</u> 1.26.2020

A Divine design
Sends shivers down my spine
And I contemplate what to do
With my time
While my eyes are opening in my mind
Bringing realizations from past times
Leaving me feeling empty and blind

My Soul's Lament 2.6.2020

My soul's constant lament
Has me crying for happiness

I strive and strive
To feel alive

The peace I should feel
Has been soured by a
Polluted deal
Thought to be my relief
But somehow combs out
My capacity
To get my emotions into reality.

A Dream's Sanity? 2.8.2020

Teetering on the edge of sanity
How do I regain
What's lost inside of me?
Did it even leave?
The love that was meant for me
My soul's everything

Am I becoming a new me?
Do I even agree?
I'm shuttering
This can't be reality
Now,
My dreams,
I'll never see
With so many possibilities
It's not worth risking.

<u>My Own Cold</u> 2.8.2020

Frantic words
Curse my soul
Sending me into my own
Abyss of cold
The murderous words
Add to the storm
My feelings are swirling
It's never-ending twirling
There are knives in my skull
Creating so much more
More,
Hatred
More,
Malice
More,
Never-ending torture

It's unrelenting
Completely heart-breaking
Distorting who I am
Into a monstrous mad
That has to be suppressed
But,
When the storm is over
I still have no answers
No closure
Just complete loss of composure.

<u>Numbing Trauma</u> 2.8.2020

The numbing is taking over
Why, do I have to remember
These memories
Are traumatizing
I feel overwhelmed
With anxiety

Feelings of hatred are beginning to form
"These are no longer dangerous concerns"
Yet,
The disturbance I feel
I cannot conceal
I need to stay away
But,
That's not the way to behave
According to those
Who do not know,
These memories welling up
Are all just too much.

Even After 2.20.2020

When you try to rip
Sanity away from me
And tear my heart
To make it bleed
Even after,
You've heard my reasoned plea
Only then, you will see
The monster hiding in me
The screaming, cursed weapon
I need
To help me feel
I am worth something.

Sadness and Strength 2.23.2020

Twisting torment
Bringing a terrifying lament
This sadness
Is creating madness
Yet,
Retrieving happiness
At the simplest extent
Self-love is coming evident
But,
The torture slows
My ability
To break this hold on me
The delusions are taunting me
Making it hard
To even want to breathe
If I step out
The strength I need now
Might not be found.

Rip my Heart 2.23.2020

It's like they rip my heart away
Then curse me with what I say
Although, I can be blamed
Should they really tempt fate?
The things I say
May take evil shape
But truth,
Is in these mistakes
No matter which side you take.

<u>Haunted Fairytale</u> 3.8.2020

I'm just so delusional
Lost in a fairytale
With haunting wedding bells
I don't know how I fell
Did I have control?
He had me in his spell
This is a twisted Hell
Yet,
So pleasurable,
It restores me
But, now my fears are circling
Around my head
I hope I don't end up dead

What could this be?
Is it all Insanity?

Tortured Days 4.11.2020

This sickening way
Is disturbance,
Torturing my days
Taking all my dignity
Wrapping all around me
Becoming all encompassing
Thrashing my sanity
Keeping me wandering
Is this monster,
Just inside me?

Hope? 4.11.2020

Is there hope?
I'm losing how I cope
It's driving me to the brink
I'm fighting for sanity
In my mind's boxing ring

The depression from this tragedy
Is taking a hold of me
I need
To regain control of everything
And have a reason to live.

I need to look at the small things
And remember the joy they bring.
Although,
With no song to sing,
I fear,
I'll lose everything.

Melancholy Melody 4.25.2020

The melody of my soul
Is melancholy and untold
I am an old soul
Gaining wisdom as I grow
Appearances I dismiss
But now I see that as a trick
Teaching me the wrong way
While I try to explain.

Fading Days 4.25.2020

The time weaves together
In my mind's shelter
The days just fade away
With all my shame
Though, I'm feeling better
Then before
I'm still so insecure
I need a cure
It's dark and dismal
Can I regain what they stole?
They really can't kill my soul
Will I make it through the melodies
Of the cold?

Burdened and Bruised 4.25.2020

I'm burdened and bruised
Feeling lost and used
Manipulated by those consumed
The chaos, they ensue
Will never bring the new
My future,
I can't grasp
The present,
Makes me gasp
How sick is this world?
Am I delusional?
I ask
As everything takes me back
To a time, I need to forget.

Pleasure and Peace 5.1.2020

This demon
Supposedly,
Came to save me
But is leaving me empty
And feeling violated
My mind invaded
My soul feels taken
My reality has been morphed
Into something so warped
My soul is torn
Between pleasure and peace
Do I need this to cease?
It's not reality
So why play make believe
In this twisted life,
I might leave.

Death and Peace 5/1/2020

Death and peace
Circle around me
What is reality?
The darkness that surrounds
Tries to steal my sounds
And make it
Its own
Stealing my show
Trying to make me grow cold
This feeling in my bones
Is heavy,
And not my own
It's a swirling darkness
Leading to torn bliss
Of love and happiness
A delusion created by my mind
Rendering me blind
I can't see the way to go
I'm trying to get through this
Grey smoke
Why, oh, why can't I end this show?

My Happiness's Romance 5.2.2020

Demons dancing in my dreams
Are terrorizing me
Why can't I see
What their intentions are for me?
Is it to help me breathe,
Or destroy me?
I'm seriously grasping
To a reality
That could utterly
Cause me to break
But,
There's a chance
My happiness's romance
Will bring a life with bliss
I hope,
That's what I don't miss.

<u>Harmonious Rhymes</u> 5.25.2021

My Soul and my time
Are intertwined
With a harmonious rhyme
That I can't help but give my life
This blessed curse
Undoes my universe
These artistic reaches
Scream,
Keep your distance!
Scaring my soul
Sending me into an infinite cold
Chilling my untouched bones
Molding me into something spiritual
Not quite real
Twisted at its core
Just an evil, never-ending curse

Is this a necessity?
Because right now I need the comforting
This dark bliss
Creates a certain warmth
And it feels like my heart
Has finally dispersed.

<u>Soothe and Save</u> 6.19.2020

This melancholy soul of mine
Lets the notes soothe and save my mind
From a tortuous illness
Stealing any of my progress

Throughout this torment
It's been a ruthless constant
Quelling,
Yet,
Torturing.
Everything I'm remembering
Into a state of bliss
I'm forced to dismiss.

Demon Inside? 6.19.2020

This demon lurking inside me
Is mesmerizing
Helping me forget everything
That's haunting me
That empties me

I try to flee
But it holds me
Embraces me tenderly
It seems insane
But, it helps me turn the page.

Is this an angel in disguise?
Showing me my life?
Helping me to find
Peace of mind
When I died.

The Times 6.19.2020

Seduced by the times
I begin to fly
This love makes me high
So, why do I cry?
Because it's a lie.

Seduced by the times

Bleeding Darkness 6.20.2020

The darkness bleeds
Through everything
Enrapturing me and causing
Reality to leave
With chains that are binding me
To something blinding
Completely enveloping
It's a disguise of happiness
Causing a blackened bliss
It's my soul's poisonous kiss
Creating my fantasy
While killing me internally
Wrapping around all corners of me
Digging out and emptying
Too many feelings
Returning me to
A human being.

Night 6.28.2020

In the night of my mind
The dark swirls
It's a raging storm
That makes me blind

Reality gets altered
And everything is backward
All love is gone
And I am nothing but flawed.

No one wants me alive
They want suicide
And I'm told that's a lie
But,
How do I prove that?
Through all skepticism
When hatred,
Is all that's in my vision.

<u>Love or Delusions?</u> 6.30.2020

The brain can do funny things
It can make you believe
A reality
That does not exist
It can reach into vast emptiness
And bring out torture
That doesn't relent
It can create a delusion
Of love that feels God sent.
But,
Leaves you with nothing but hollowness
Just trying to grasp
How your brain can lead you
Into a trap
That hurts and bruises
Always confuses
Love for delusions.

<u>Hallucinations</u> 7.2.2020

Enrapturing my mental desire
Adding fuel to my fire
Bending my will
Changing my views
Leaving me questioning you
But still begging for truth.

I've never known this kind of desire
You are my sire
Exposing me
To the purity
Within the feelings
The peaceful longing and needing
That leaves my soul believing
This is worth feeling.

Abnormal? 7.8.2020

Happiness...

Does it even exist?
I think I see it
In those who believe in it
But, is it the truth in private?
Am I really more abnormal?
Than them?

<u>Torturing Myself to Love</u> 7.8.2020

Love escapes me
In my heart and externally
This cold heart I've held
Is trying to warm itself
The storm it leads me to
Tortures me into breakthroughs
I suppose, I resist
Even though, it'll lead me to my heart's bliss
It's hard to stop this defensiveness
And that's where to the torture begins.

Untitled 7.8.2020

Love...
What's it for?
Can it really restore?
Does it exist?
Or is it just a dream of bliss?

My Minds Puzzle 7.8.2020

My mind's suppression
Is a necessary measure
I cannot live
In a reality
That destroys me
And causes panic with a
Need to leave
I need patience to keep waiting
Waiting to be restored.

With every piece of the puzzle
I'll put it all together
And search for happiness forever.

Singing to Live 7.9.2020

The nature of man
Is something
I no longer understand
The world displays
We should not act with cruelty
Yet,
Everyone I've met
Has sought to ruin me
Or
Is this just what I perceive?
Confusion is what I believe
Never knowing anything
But,
When I'm singing
I can be sure of one thing
Life can be worth living.

<u>Lowering My Defenses</u> 7.15.2020

Watch the tar-stained walls
As I fall
Black ink
Sinks in
As I drink the poison
My life is turning
Revolving
I might be healing
But,
This sickness
Stops the process
Leaves me lifeless
Rendering me useless
Barely functioning
It's trying to stop my questioning
Stopping the reason, I'm living
Stopping the confrontations
Ending my long-standing situation
Of emotional frustration
Sending me into volcanic eruptions
But,
Watch as I lower my defenses
Will this be how I end it?

Can't Handle 7.18.2020

Emptiness has taken over
When will this be over?
My mental torture
When will I feel better?
From everything I can't seem
To handle.
It's an overwhelming pressure
And surrounds my mental state
Making me lose everything that's
At stake
Changing me into a monstrous debate
But only internally,
Because,
It's laughable to believe
Anyone cares for me.

Divine Vengeance 7.18.2020

This vengeance circling around me
Is all encompassing
Changing my mind
Rendering me blind
Releasing what's mine
It's almost divine
It opens my eyes
Leading me out of my disguise.

<u>Panicked Reactions</u> 7.18.2020

The panic that
Causes me to react
Leaves sadness
I need to suppress
My life has been laid to rest
I feel them attack
Their love,
Is what I lack
And when I try to escape
They surround and try to take
My soul tries to flee
Tries to hold onto anything
To make life worth living.

<u>Devastation</u> 7.21.2020

In the wake of my devastation
I'm left with nothing but frustration
And very little to believe in

The emptiness I feel is cold
The darkness is taking ahold
I feel I'm in a dampened room
Just cowering from the view
The room is blue and gray
And I fade into the shades
Torturing myself
On how to behave
While feeling nothing but pain.

If Only 7.27.2020

Eventually love blooms
But it can consume
And this
Is why it can be toxic to you.

This is the reason
Love, I can't believe in
It can't be in my vision
This would be detrimental to my mind's living
I feel it could end everything
If only love was real
And not just a fairytale.

<u>My Heart's Passion</u> 7.27.2020

I feel high above the pain
It must be the adrenaline
I feel I'm floating
Almost gloating
Just knowing
The truth of me,
Is not for them to see.

It's good I closed down
They've taken all they could
And left town
But,
They didn't see my heart's longing
It was lying dormant
Just finishing its time to ferment
To really grow
Into the passion
I love and know.

Hard Left 7.27.2020

My life took a hard left
But even through all this mess
Maybe,
It's for my best
It's a return home
Singing melodies from the soul
I don't know how or where to go
I need to figure it out on my own
But,
This demented show
Distorts my dreams
Underestimates me
And I begin to believe
I am NOTHING.

<u>Poisonous Brain</u> 7.28.2020

Poisons, poisons
Flowing from my brain
Driving me insane
What is this never-ending game?
Showing and expanding my shame
Into a torturous distortion
Stealing my portion
It's trying to create a monster
That I will not follow
Even though, this curse is
Within
I know my path can conflict
This ailment
And I will live.

Amusement 8.2.2020

What was I thinking?
I don't need this
He is poison in my dreams
Chaining me to this insane reality
Coaxing my thoughts
To things I could want
Stealing the truth
Trying to make his move
Trying to collapse my universe
Trying to make me into a morbid curse
This will not work.

Spiders 8.9.2020

Spiders swirling towards me
Twisting my mind and taunting
Do I even have a chance to flee?
They're surrounding
I'm falling
They're crawling
All over my bones
All over the pain I don't show
The love I don't want them to know
Now,
I find myself slipping lower
In this game of torture
Decisions I'm making
Make me feel forsaken
By God and man
I feel I'm doing all I can
The problem is,
It's not enough.
I really just want to give up.

Dimensions 8.11.2020

I feel young and helpless
Trapped between dimensions
One reality
Scares me
But, the sensations won't
Let me leave
And it's sickening
The other reality
Bores me
But,
Will it help me breathe?

Untitled 8.15.2020

What is love to me?
It's a dream
Way out of reach
It's not tangible to me
So,
Why for others, does it come so easy?
It's really me I'm manipulating
By hiding my feelings
It's what makes me uneasy
Like love is what I'm missing.

Harmonies 8.15.2020

The harmonies pour out of me
My mouth intertwines with my soul
Bringing blissful feelings
That momentarily steal all the cold
I truly feel warmth
It's an inside glow
That is all my own

It's changing my path's direction
I can't seem to help it
It makes my soul free
And helps me soar above the agony
This feels like the only thing
To believe in
It's consuming
Every inch of me
But,
Since it makes me happy
Why can't it be in my ending?

<u>Smoldering Past</u> 8.20.2020

I'm walking through smoldering ashes
Guided by past actions
My feet have this
But, my brain is not relaxing
Then,
I stare into the coals
And get hypnotized by their lost souls
They're burning my conscious mind
Into chaos and paranoia
That leaves me lost in time
The present moment
Cannot come into focus
Leaving me enraptured
By moments I did not capture.

<u>Smoke</u> 8.25.2020

Smoke flows out
In the perfect amount
It's like water
A breath that doesn't make
It harder
This unhealthy crutch
Will always have me stuck
Because,
When the smoke flows out
I don't feel without.

<u>Lost</u> 8.28.2020

Where have I been?
My soul has been lost
In a delusional wonderland
With harmonies filling
All the emotions I've kept hidden
The love I was constantly stealing
It was a device of my own
A torturing show
Leaving my mind afloat
Hovering above
My own conscious awareness
Making my life completely useless.

<u>Depressed</u> 9.6.2020

I'm uninspired
And so tired
Drained by the fires
Fires,
In my brain
Illuminating
Everything I've tried to save
Every piece of me
That keeps me grasping
To an impossible reality.

<u>Worth it?</u> 9.6.2020

This road I led myself down
Filled with demonic, laughing clowns
Seemed the perfect avenue
To get rid of all I've been through
But, somehow,
I became confused
This demulcent distortion
Makes me wonder...

Am I worth anything?
When my past is consuming
Every ember I'm leaving
To bring back my being
The trail is disintegrating
Am I worth saving?

Route of My Soul 9.15.2020

The route of my soul
Will help my beauty unfold
The melody humming inside
Is a longing to shine
A longing of love
That gives my heart a shove
To delight in a prospect
Of a better life
Even if it doesn't look quite right
It's better than my continuous night.

<u>War</u> 9.19.2020

You say "bite your tongue"
But I say "this war is not yet won"
There are choices in view
Leading me down different avenues

Which choice is right?
Which is not a venomous bite?

It's time to take a step back

With previous experience
Leading me out of this torment
Victory; I can almost taste it
When will I be able to end this?

<u>Traumatizing Intimacy</u> 10.3.2020

The word intimacy
Has me cringing
But,
Please don't judge me
I'm only a human being
Affected by my surroundings
And the trauma I've seen
Turning loving actions
Into something I can't fathom

Traumatizing me
With normalcy
Few can continue comprehending
This line of thinking.

My Way 10.6.2020

This is my way of journaling
With all this ink I bleed
All these words surround me
Stealing away my mood's gravity
Giving me that release
These rhymes leave my mind floating
They give me a break from depressed
Feelings
With what I'm creating

The weight of the words
Goes down like a written curse
Releasing all I've rehearsed
All the trivial pain
I indulge in daily
That leaves me drowning
But,
This writing
Pulls me back
And keeps me grounded.

<u>Worth it?</u> 10.16.2020

My soul is only free
In the midst of insanity
But,
It can't be worth comprehending
It scares me blind
It scares me with all that lies behind
Reliving every moment
Feeling everything, I regret
Again, and again
It comes back
To live and stay
Back, to my tortured stage
Back, to my show
That always leaves me cold
And alone.

Suicide...
It seems the only way to fix my life
It storms my mind
leaves my hopeless in time
The army within
Cannot conquer these feelings
Every day I'm drowning
Suicide...
Continues to be tempting
Maybe, then, I'll forget everything
Nothing gets left behind
I need to stop the memories
Running my life
I get lost in moments inside
Then suicidal thoughts return
And I want to end all I've learned
Will I be haunted forever?
These memories are what I need to sever.

Feelings of Love 11.11.2020

These feelings that storm my brain
Are terrifying
While confusing
Thoughts of love.
While,
Non-existent
Are severely persistent
And I'm trying to find a way around it
But then,
I stop to question
Does this need mending?
Am I cold hearted?
Am I going to finish this process?
Will I change?
To enjoy love's name
Stop living in shame
For the most normal things.

<u>Meant to Win</u> 11.23.2020

I'm not settling
The love must be
All encompassing
Pulling every inch of me
Into all I need
To help me breathe
Meant to be
Only for me
No one else
Can come in between
Such a rarity
Just me and him
Someone my heart lets win.

<u>Closed Eyes</u> 12.4.2020

"How does it feel, to destroy a life?"
I utter as I close my eyes
Is everyone this blind?
How do they not know what's right?

Fearful Ideas 12.4.2020

It gets its ideas
From my fears
Reducing me to tears
Torturing me through the years
Giving the demons
Rise to what they believe in
Torturing my body and soul
Trying to turn me cold
Taking my sanity
And my vanity
I can't even see my face
Where's the beauty
God meant to create
It's plain morbid
These mindful distortions
Could they be a life lesson?
I suppose, I'll keep on guessing.

Negative Positivity 12.4.2020

Treading above emptiness
Trying to proceed with happiness
Yet,
Negativity swallows me
It's all I can seem to bleed
And all I ever seem to need
Depression is closing in
I fear this won't end
How twisted it seems
This negative positivity.

<u>Nieve?</u> 12.9.2020

You make me feel like I'm being saved
You're unrelenting on this stage
Twirling me around
Changing what's to be found
Into beauty
I never knew I needed
I was blind and tormented
Believing
No one could love me
Let alone,
My own love being shown
Could this really be
A good thing?

Am I In Hell? 12.9.2020

Things are getting hazy
This can't be my reality
This asylum has me questioning
Am I alive?
Am I in Hell?
All my fears have come to dwell
It's a nightmare that never ends
All I can do is play pretend
I'm so scared
I don't know what's real
Why am I going through this?
How can this be how I live?

You Saved My Life 12.12.2020

My heart is heavy
Losing you,
Has me regretting
And feeling unsteady
 I loved you beyond words
And now life has taken you
For good.
I don't know how to move on
It just seems wrong.

You saved my life
Too many times
When I thought I should die
You'd give me that light
I needed by my side
To keep me alive.
I can't let you go
Without you I have no home.
But,
To honor your memory
I will continue on
Until God says
"Come Home."

<u>A Fight</u> 12.12.2020

A fight
For my soul
A fight
Turning me from the cold
A fight
Bringing longing out of me
It's all I can see
The love that's blinding
Will it rescue me?
This supposed love in my sea.

<u>Consequences</u> 12.12.2020

I no longer know how to live
With all these consequences
That have come into existence
Ruining all I believe in
Taking everything, I live for.

Behavioral Lies 12.15.2020

The rumbling skies
Push the turmoil inside
To a place where it will rise
I will scare your heart and eyes
With my behavioral lies
This is why
No one stays by my side
Even though, they're worse than my kind.
Love;
Does it even exist?
With backstabbers and traitors
In my midst
Why should I behave better?
When they think they're so clever?
My life is already gone
So,
Here lie
All my flaws.

Inspired Virus 12.15.2020

This inspired virus
Was their device
To torture my mind
And drive me inside
Inside, my disguise
Keeping me there
Never letting me repair
Wanting me to maintain
Yet,
They're pushing me to live in vain
Angry, bitter, and broken
This is what they have spoken.

<u>Darkness</u> 12.30.2020

This dark street
This torturous agony
My soul's mystery
Keeps me encaged in misery
Just longing for the notes
To soothe my soul
And my real nature to unfold
To become my own.

<u>Lenses</u> 12.30.2020

No one sees good in me
Through the lens of my insanity
The only reality
They want to see
Is where I'm a villain
Lost in emotion
Always a burden
They're lost in what I've misspoken
Leaving me feeling
Like sickness is winning
This must be the end and not beginning
I long for healing
And reality given
But no one sees
They let my illness define me
And that is why they always leave.

Knowing Love 12.30.2020

I've been questioning
Has there ever
Been love inside me
While I struggle with this disease
I'm broken and empty
Losing all hope,
 I've been holding
Just knowing
My days are dissolving
And no one is calling
Every regret
That brought torment
Is consuming all I lament
I can't see past this indifference
The love,
They'll never give
In any instance.

Final Cost

Reality;
I use this word a lot
But,
With sickness
It's all you've got
And yet,
It's all that's lost
And is the final cost.

The End... For now.